OF EARTHLY PARADISE

*To Julia —
Once again!
with much love
from
Ane

3·xii·92
School of Pythagoras*

Also by Clive Wilmer

POETRY

The Dwelling-Place 1977
Devotions 1982

TRANSLATIONS (with George Gömöri)

Forced March: Selected Poems of Miklós Radnóti 1979
*Night Song of the Personal Shadow: Selected Poems
of György Petri* 1991

EDITIONS

Thom Gunn: *The Occasions of Poetry* 1982
John Ruskin: *Unto this Last & Other Writings* 1985
Dante Gabriel Rossetti: *Selected Poems and Translations* 1991
William Morris: *News from Nowhere & Other Prose Writings* (forthcoming)
George Herbert: *Selected Writings* (forthcoming)

Clive Wilmer
Of Earthly Paradise

CARCANET

First published in Great Britain in 1992 by
Carcanet Press Limited
208-212 Corn Exchange Buildings
Manchester M4 3BQ

Copyright © Clive Wilmer 1992
The right of Clive Wilmer to be identified as the
author of this work has been asserted by him in
accordance with the Copyright, Designs and Patents
Act of 1988.
All rights reserved

A CIP catalogue record for this book is
available from the British Library
ISBN 0 85635 978 5

The publisher acknowledges financial assistance
from the Arts Council of Great Britain

Set in 10½ pt Sabon by Bryan Williamson, Darwen
Printed and bound in England by SRP Ltd, Exeter

To the Memory of my Mother

K.S.W. (1904-1985)

Alive, I could not write for you, who dead
Live in the words you planted in my head.

ACKNOWLEDGEMENTS

Some of these poems have already appeared elsewhere. Thanks are due to the editors, publishers and broadcasters concerned.

'Wild Flowers', 'Bindweed Song' and 'An Autumn Vision' appeared in my previous Carcanet collection, *Devotions*. They now find their place in the sequence *A Catalogue of Flowers*, which was published as a limited edition by Robert L. Barth. Other poems have appeared in two further limited editions: *Amores* (Leslie Bell) and *The Infinite Variety* (Barth).

Several poems have appeared in festschrifts and anthologies. These include: *First and Always* (Faber), *The Music of his History* (Barth), *A Few Friends* (Stonyground Press), *Nine Years After* (Barth), *A Garland for John Finlay* (Blue Heron Press) and *Order and Variety* (University of Delaware). Others have appeared in these periodicals: *Agenda, Cambridge Poetry Magazine, Cambridge Review, Critical Quarterly, Cumberland Poetry Review, Drastic Measures, Ideas and Production, London Review of Books, Modern Painters, Pequod, PN Review, Poetry Durham, Spectator, Threepenny Review*. 'Cattle Market' and 'At the Grave of Ezra Pound' were broadcast on *Poetry Now* (BBC Radio 3).

Contents

1
Invocation | 11
Three Brueghel Paintings | 13
St Francis Preaching to the Birds | 14
The San Damiano Crucifix | 15
The Coat of Many Colours | 16
Cattle Market | 17
Birdsong and Polyphony | 19
The Infinite Variety | 20
The Thirst | 23
To Robert Wells | 24

2 *A Catalogue of Flowers*
Wild Flowers | 27
Bindweed Song | 28
An Autumn Vision | 29
Post-War Childhoods | 30
Conservancy | 32
Alkanet | 34
To Paint a Salt Marsh | 35

3
Work | 39
The Law of the House | 42
At the Grave of Ezra Pound | 43
At the Grave of William Morris | 44
Fonte Branda in Siena | 45
To a Poet from Eastern Europe, 1988 | 46
To Haydn and Mozart | 47
The Kitchen Table | 48

4
Charon's Bark | 51
Two Journals | 52
The Temple of Aphrodite | 53
Amores | 56
Re-reading my Poem 'Saxon Buckle' | 59
Transference | 60
The Dream | 61
In the Greenwood | 62
The Garden | 63
Oasis | 64
The Earth Rising | 65

5 *Versions*
Caedmon's Hymn | 69
Canticle of the Sun (St Francis) | 70
Sestina (Dante) | 72
Dante to Love's Faithful | 74
Cavalcanti's Reply | 75
Archaic Torso of Apollo (Rilke) | 76
'Say, poet, what it is you do' (Rilke) | 77
Caedmon of Whitby | 78

1

Invocation

Unanswering voice,
Sustainer,
Lady or Lord:
I have no choice
But to attend
Your silent word.

I think again
Of the first poet
Of our tongue:
Abandoning
The sweet, profane
Intoxication
Of plucked string
And exploit sung.

At your command
He sang creation.

He had withdrawn
To where
His silence was:
Where cattle stand
And, sleeping, moan,
Stamp, grumble, snort.

As in high places dawn
Will spring
Sudden from stone,
So from the dung
And bed-straw rose
His made thought.

Angel or Muse,
Because I do
Not hear your voice
Yet cannot choose
But speak, I pray

Let my words be
Such that they grow
From my silence
Answering you,
As they
Must answer me.

Three Brueghel Paintings

The Massacre of the Innocents
The Conversion of St Paul
Hunters in the Snow

I

This is the world (the painter says)
Reduced by ice and snow, bone-bare.
    Then ride in mercenaries.
Armed to the teeth, they introduce
    Fear, panic and despair.
They'd trace a king. How can they know
        He is not here?

II

Where earth encounters heaven, cloud
Frays on the trees that spike the air.
    Ranks crumble to a crowd
Of stragglers. Some, bemused and dazed
    By light's intrusion, stare
At one the light has felled, who sees
        What is not there.

III

No myth informs this wintry view
Enhanced by no nostalgic care
    For skies of southern blue.
Skaters delight in circumstance
    Three hunters come to share,
Who slant against winds charged with snow
        From who knows where.

St Francis Preaching to the Birds
for Tamsin

Not angels these; although
Their melody and flight
Subsume the world, their wings
Substantiating light.

This man whom inwardness
And gracious thought have blessed,
Possessing nothing, knows
Both ear and eye possessed.

Their being crowds against
His gates of sense: to move
Into the mind, where language
Declares the movement love,

Though love is his, not theirs.
They, living beyond reach,
Indifferent to meaning,
Are made anew in speech.

The San Damiano Crucifix
which spoke to St Francis

A church about to fall.
The saint of poverty
Knelt in the church to pray,
Loving its poverty.

Flesh-tint and gold leaf
Hung there above him: a cross.
With bodily ears he heard
A voice speak from the cross

In pain, exhorting him
Repair my broken House.
Stone by stone he repaired
The body of that house:

For though the letter kills,
The spirit and the word
Move in the flesh alone.
So too, although the words

Spoken by painted wood
And answered in his work
May not be what we hear,
It is a speaking work.

The Coat of Many Colours

Do not interpretations
belong to God?

Joseph: Rich colour signifies deep inwardness.
The bending sheaves, the sun's the moon's decline
Are colours in this coat, my father's gift.
Some bleed and blend. Others, like potentates,
Stand out – see! – urgent and peremptory.

One of the All his tall stories, dreams he calls them, stress
brothers: His own pre-eminence, its outward sign
That coat he swaggers in... What but that gift
Has he to show?... How his pretension grates,
The smugness posing as authority!

Potiphar's My mordant lust, no matter what he says,
wife: He woke in me. Now I dream his body's line,
Its nervous thrust imprisoned, and the gift
Of so reading desire his eye translates
– Through cold reflection – heat to chastity.

Pharaoh: Amun, we are all, gaudy or poor our dress,
Rich with an inwardness that seals us thine!
I raise this man to greatness for a gift
Beyond such wealth, since what his night creates
His day interprets with lucidity.

Jacob: I dreamt you had not gone, though dreamt it less
The nearer death I grew. O son of mine,
Now I have found you, death shall be a gift,
And dream and understanding the twin gates
I pass through as I near reality.

Cattle Market

for Gabriel

Why brook'st thou, ignorant beast, subjection?
Why dost thou, bull and boar, so seelily
Dissemble weakness, and by one man's stroke die
Whose whole kind you might swallow and feed upon?
                                                    Donne

Seely or silly?
            Timorous beasts
Thwacked and buffeted into pens
Clamour against the world, although
The hands they suffer at are men's.
Terror masters them – it protests,
Seems to resist, then lets them go

Lambs to the slaughter, pigs, cows...
Men who stand and look on equate
Value with fleshly substance – price
The measure of it; and this they state
By way of nods and puckering brows.
Yet the whole place seems paradise

To one of them, who does not count
Or bid, through whom a passion stares
And feeds on what he cannot grasp:
Each penned or passing creature wears,
For him, an auric splendour, faint
But clear and there. His fingers clasp

A hand above him, trembling at
The power a solicitous father bends
To shield him from. But through the boy's
Passion – uncertain where it tends,
What it might mean – the man has caught
Something of brilliance, so that he toys

With likenesses, which grope and guess
At meaning: through such wintry light
As lingers in the frosted breath
Looping these mindless skulls, one might
(He fancies) look on blessedness.
What moves him though, beyond all myth,

Is what the bidders, were they to break
Silence, might judge beneath contempt –
The vacant, dumb docility
With which most other lives are stamped.
This powerlessness to choose or speak
So fleshes out the verb *to be*

That children innocent of pain
Take it for glory: which, absurd
To traders who provide for them,
Seems emblem of a fate endured
To those who dream of angels on
The darkened hills of Bethlehem.

Christmas Eve, 1983

Birdsong and Polyphony

The birds in this illuminated manuscript –
Wood-dove and song-thrush, chaffinch and goldfinch –
Are radiant marginalia that gloss
The notion of music, the notation of music.

We take it that their natural artifice
Would drench creation in polyphony;
They perch at the white borders of the page,
The score behind them, held back from flight.

The Infinite Variety

1. *The Museum of Natural History, Santa Barbara*
   (for Edgar Bowers)

All the birds of the region in one room,
Condor to humming-bird! Only a glance takes in
Pelican, golden eagle, blue-jay, wren...
Two hundred maybe, stuffed, posed, poised for flight.
What need (you say) has nature for so many
Exquisite variations? She selects
Each kind, are we to think, by fine distinction –
In the whole country, say, some forty species
Of warbler, each a different intersection
Of colour, music, mass, texture and form?
Or was it some such randomness as jars
Through the San Andreas Fault, which will in time
Shatter this state of high prosperity
To nameless this and that: did some such flaw
Cause these named rifts, that branch in plenitude?

2. Minerals from the collection of John Ruskin

The boy geologist who clove the rocks
Here on display grew up to be the great
Philosopher of colour into form
And, in the products of just workmanship,
Discerned the paradigm of the just state.

It was the Lord's design he made apparent –
These bands and blocks of azure, umber, gilt,
Set in their flexing contours, solid flow
That had composed itself in its own frame:
Red garnet neighbouring mica, silver white;
A slice of agate like an inland sea...

In manhood, similarly, his eye judged how
Good stone splits fairly at the mason's touch;
How painters stay their colour, shape the run
And blotch of it to images of truth.
He taught that these, and others like them, might
– Workers with hand or mind – be driven less
By harsh need or harsh fate than by the call
Imagination hears to make new worlds:
Which honour in epitome this world,
Ruled by its fluid and elusive forms.

If chance be providential, the taught eyes
Of those who paint or carve so should instruct us
In justice and original design.

3. *My father's collection of Indian butterflies and moths*

   (for Val)

I have no names for them, foreign to me,
Although my father named and numbered each.
Nor, now they are gone, can I recall
One individual insect – neither shape
Nor colour nor composition. So I brood
On formless memories of moths so big
They looked like two splayed hands linked at the thumbs,
And butterflies arranged by deviation
From an unstated norm of their design:
You could imagine them – they were so vibrant –
Cut from some miniature of Shah Jahan's.

I was three when my father died; my mother
Outlived him forty years. When she died too,
My sister and I brought down the insect boxes –
Perhaps in expectation that that vision
Of plenitude, long stowed, awaited us.
I could not breathe to think of them. We opened
To nothing but a hint of dust, and pins
Staked upright, row on row, like monuments
To that which he had left us, though it felt
As if what he had left us had not been.

The Thirst

A kingfisher darting the green scum on a pool
Leaves it unbroken. Out of and over long grass
An erratic career, and a hare has become distance.

These things should be enough. But the old Adam
In me calls for their naming, seeing in them
Not at all more than their being there, but more
Than that they are. The one lust we can never
Wholly contain. The one unquenchable thirst.

The body barely withdrawn from the spring of delight,
And a full silence. Unbroached it cannot be.

To Robert Wells

on his translation of The Georgics

This is your poem of fields and flocks and trees
(As it was Virgil's) for the words are yours,
If words are of a poet, which are ours
And not ours either but the names of things.

2
A Catalogue of Flowers

Wild Flowers

Ragwort and mallow, toadflax and willow herb
Trick out the wasteground patchwork that I thread
To no end, not for delight, but with a passion
Such as they feel who are obsessed with death –

Though this is not death. I linger here
Where rot assumes these terrace-house cadavers,
And brick-rubble, riven paving-slabs, puddled ruts
Are cordoned off by bindweed tapestries

On looms of fence-wire. One might think neglect
Cultivates that for which it has made way –
The minor glories idleness in passing
Name: 'wallflower', 'dogrose', maybe 'traveller's joy'.

Bindweed Song

    I am convolvulus.
I prosper where your ways are undermined
By war or social lapse. So call me weed:
Bindweed that comes uncalled for, weeds that bind.

    Where eyesores are I flourish –
Where mildew, rat and spider occupy
Your seat and artefact. They are the world,
You the ephemerids, and what am I

    Who have wound a way back in?
– Who mesh and drape (until they all cohere)
Hedge, pathway and door-frame. See, passer-by,
How beauty decks the substance of your fear.

An Autumn Vision

    In dreams, in bombed-out houses,
      Where childhood used to play,
   Among brambles and briar roses
And grass running to seed I pick my way,

    Until I reach a clearing
    Of strafed and harrowed ground
  Where tombs founder, smoke blackened,
Corroded angels mourning, and no sound.

   Finding the grave – a broadsword
    Laid on memorial loam
 As the tomb cross – and leaning forward
To gouge the sooty lichen from a name,

  I glimpse beyond in the greenwood
    Some purple artifice
(A helmet plume?) flourishing over
The drawn, despairing, honourable face

    Of one whose quest advances
    Down broken paths that tend
  Towards a past locked in battle
With wrong he knows no future can amend.

Post-War Childhoods

for Takeshi Kusafuka

If there were no affliction in this world we might think we were in paradise.
                Simone Weil, Gravity and Grace

You, born in Tokyo
In nineteen forty-four,
Knew the simplicity
Occasioned by a war.
In London it was so
Even in victory –
In defeat, how much more.

Knew it I say – and yet,
Born to it, you and I,
How could we in truth have known?
It was the world. You try
To make articulate,
In language not your own,
What it was like and why.

Nature returned (you say)
To downtown Tokyo –
In your voice, some irony
Defending your need to go
That far: what other way
Of like economy
Is there of saying so?

Your images declare
The substance of the phrase:
Bomb craters, urban grass,
A slowworm flexing the gaze
Of the boy crouching there;
Moths, splayed on the glass,
Like hands lifted in praise.

A future might have drawn
On what such things could tell.
You heard, even as you woke,
Accustomed birdsong fill
The unpolluted dawn,
Heard a toad blurt and croak
In some abandoned well.

They call it desolation,
The bare but fertile plot
You have been speaking of.
You grew there, who have taught
Me much of the relation
Affliction bears to love
In Simone Weil's scoured thought.

I, too, have images.
A photograph: St Paul's,
The dome a helmeted head
Uplifted, as terror falls.
The place I knew, not this
But a city back from the dead,
Grew fireweed within walls.

I played over dead bombs
In suburban villas, a wrecked
Street of them where, run wild,
Fat rhododendrons cracked
The floors of derelict rooms:
It seemed to a small child
An Eden of neglect.

If we two share a desire,
It is not that either place,
Still less the time, should return.
If gravity and grace
Survive a world on fire
Fixed in the mind, they burn
For things to be in peace.

Conservancy

for Heather Glen

It was the treatment of the banks by the Thames Conservancy Board, which regularly cut down all the flowers and cleared the stream of its pleasant flowering reeds and rushes, which so enraged Morris.

Philip Henderson, *William Morris*

"These were the buds that tipped desire
And shaped what might be from what is.
Now summer grants the river's edge
This wealth of colour: bullrushes,

Long purples, a strong yellow flower
That's close and buttony, horse mint,
Mouse ear, belated meadow-sweet,
And dark blue mug-wort – not a hint

Of luxury in the excess
That freshens in the passing gust,
Or anarchy in the design
Of that which grows where grow it must.

Yet now the Thames Conservancy,
Subversive of this perfect state,
Instructs the servile ministers
Of order to annihilate

These frail entanglements, this fine
Community of loveliness,
Where natural harmony, though not
Traceable, governs nonetheless.

I loose my anger, then withdraw
To dream the paradise within:
Rich banks of colour that declare
Proudly a humble origin

Without – I weave them from the dark
And so, approximately, chart
The paradise we share, whose stream
Rises and rises in the heart."

Alkanet

for Di

I'd seen it before but had not heard it named:
The leaves like nettles, a blue flower that peers
Above dustbins and detritus. Called alkanet,
It's a kind of wild borage, the book says.

A year, more or less, since we moved in.
That long June evening, you having gone back
To the old house, I stayed on sanding the floor
Until I could no longer see to work,

Then for the first time left by the back way.
Anxiety dulled by labour, conscious alone
Of sweat and dust and my limbs' weight, I felt
The quiet that is exhaustion coming on

And in the alley, among dark shapes of leaf –
Palpable shadows that I waded through,
My hands tingling – saw tiny flowers that retained
The sky's late intensity of blue.

When you got home I told you of the flowers
And of the light I'd seen them in. Since then
I know you have often thought of them as mine,
Not seeing that I cared for them as yours.

To Paint a Salt Marsh

Samphire and mare's tail and the salt marsh.

Nothing appears to have movement here
but the birds – it is where the white tern
pivots his swift course and on the tideline
dunlin and sandpiper dibble.
                              Otherwise,
at low tide, it's as if the brown sea
clogged in the mudflats. A spar,
tall and near the vertical, splits the view.

And on the horizon a grass-thatched sand-dune
looms like a northern fell. It
lays on the water's stillness precisely
its own stillness.

3

In the sweat of thy face shalt thou eat bread, till thou return unto the ground.

Work

*For Donald Davie,
sculptor in verse*

1

Adam,
in the sweat of his brow,
ate bread.

Eve, in pain,
laboured
to bear fruit.

She spun, she wove…
Adam carved:

not that the stones
be made bread,
but rather

that (stone worked
and habitation
hewn from it)

bread be eaten,
fruit borne.

2

At the point of the chisel
what was
a block of stone
a corbel, a capital
becomes
pierced with darkness
a leafy glade
              of the forest
brought indoors

And beneath it, cut
from the general view
for God
for the swineherd your brother,
(where an acorn-cup empty
tells of the forest floor)
two pigs
           two snouts rather
rooting among leaves

3

A mullion –
cleft and branching, then
in the marble
cut leafage, un-
furling
      clear of it

Such needless beauty
the Protestant work ethic
has no time for

Though it was hand
and labour first
bowed the mason
to the task

Which issues in this praise
of the maker of leaves and stone

The Law of the House

A house of good stone
cut fair and square,
Justice the governor –

spotless, abstract,
a goddess held in common
by all people. And all

particulars too, by virtue
of being, acknowledge
her true sway. As economy

is house law, it follows
that builders should dispose
with precision – that is,

lapidary justice.
It is a scene in fresco –
equable rule

there, figured
by impartial light
and clear space. But if

the contrasted masses
move, clash, if the ground quake
and dislodge stone,

if storm
set person against
person or against thing,

what syntax in confusion
can piece together
the logic of her dark will?

At the Grave of Ezra Pound
S. Michele, Venice

1

here lies a man
of words, who in time
came to doubt their meanings

who therefore confines
himself to two words
only here

EZRA POVND

minimal
the injury done
to the white stone

none
to the earth
it rests upon

2

The spoils of a corsair –
who ranged the Mediterranean
and brought home
porphyry, alabaster, lapis lazuli
and every hue and current of veined marble.

In the bayleaves' shade
dumb now
and within earshot
of the stilled Adriatic
deaf, rests
under white marble
la spoglia, the remains.

At the Grave of William Morris

Kelmscott Churchyard

1

where you lie
        northman
your grey gable
rugg'd with lichen

roof raised above
        no walls,
soul's shelter
from the sky's bluster,

and there underneath it
        rests
that restless body
rootless among roots

2

Through the mouth and nostrils
sprouts greenery

or rime glitters
in the great beard

Desire

like ivy on a gravestone
binds him to this one place

like grass threading
the bluebells and the cowslips
braids him into it –

this holy place,
made holier by
his love of it

by his love

Fonte Branda in Siena

Ruskin, *Praeterita* III, iv, §86
Dante, *Inferno* xxx, 49-90

Fonte Branda, wrote Ruskin, *I last saw
under the same arches where Dante saw it.
He drank of it then*
                    and every time the near
pentameters of his prose recur to me,
I too see the place again:

the *loggia* of red brick, in white stone
the jutting bestial heads
                          and within,
shade and the still pool.

Whenever the Englishman went there he would find
rage at injustice,
true words that pinion falsehood and cupidity,
bitterness in the sweet spring, the hiss
of white hot metal plunged in the cool water
as he drank.
             I think of that sad face,
the charred brain behind it, the word-flow.
And in my thought, as if toward the calm
of memory, he stoops to drink.
And every time he stoops the Florentine
in his pink coat, not crowned with laurel yet,
moves into range
                 much as another's words
return to the quiet mind.

They do not see me there. But the place names
hold them in view – *Siena, Fonte Branda* –
by brimming water, on the point of speech.

To a Poet from Eastern Europe, 1988

Strong drink –
           on the bare table a neat vodka,
Innocently transparent as pure water,
Shimmers before you, with your fence of bone
(Stake shoulders, propping arms) set up around it,
    As if, out there alone,
The spirit needed body to defend it.

From where I stand, though, I can count the cost
(The soured breath, sickly flush and hollow chest)
You pay, at 45, for what you savour.
It fortifies, calms the stomach, and yet still
    – Alas! greybeard cadaver –
Consumes the body as pure spirit will.

Consider, as you waste, how we are stewards
Of our bodies, yes, yet strangely how you thrive
On the sick body politic your words
Bite into as you're bitten: how your lust
    For truth keeps you alive,
Writhing in anger, choking on disgust.

To Haydn and Mozart

You were both endowed with flair and with, no doubt,
What is called genius; but I think of you
Bent over your claviers, two men at work,
Fending off discord with your fingertips.
At work you could stay unmoved by what you knew
Of exploitation or of penury,
Uncomprehending ignorance and pride,
Loss, disappointment, pain. You turned from these
To forms your labour could not warp, because
You heard in them the possibility
Of grace, which echoes order in the mind.

The Kitchen Table

in memory of my mother

Making a home was
what you could do
best; and cookery

(the ritual at
the heart of it) you had
a kind of genius for.

So what I first
recall, thinking of you,
is a creamy table-top,

the grain etched
crude and deep, the legs
stained black, and you

at work, with rolling-pin
or chopping-board or
bowl; then, later,

presiding over
guests or children at each
day's informal feast.

Your homeliness
displaced now, what survives
for me of it

is this: which
now becomes a model
of true art:

bare boards scrubbed clean,
black, white,
good work as grace, such

purity of heart.

4

Charon's Bark

to my Mother

1

It's the being left behind
I can't believe:
me stranded on this shore
and glimpsing you,
too far out, too baffled by the crowd
of they might be twittering shoppers,
to notice that I stay.

I recognise you by
a look of panic, so faint
who else in the world would notice it,
as you stare back at the shore,
your set eyes blind to the same look
in these that reach out after you.

2

On nights like this,
when with snow piled deep it is
too cold to snow any more
in the bitter wind,
I can't get the thought of you out of my mind.

What I keep thinking of
is waking too early on a bright morning,
and running to your bed, and jumping in.

On nights like this,
I can't keep the tears back
at the thought of you –
out there in the dark, the snow your coverlet,
unwakably asleep.

Two Journals

I keep two journals. In the first one there's
A record of dreams, fantasies and fears
That edge me toward that commonplace, the Brink:
My evidence, that is, for beak or shrink.

On odd days in the second – now more odd,
Alas, than ordinary – I brood on God,
The distant prospect of his love, and bend
Aesthetics and poetics to that end.

Sadly I can't conflate them in one text.
There I am crazed, erratic, oversexed,
Here pure, serene and earnest in my quest;
An angel here, there a tormented beast!

So when I write in one, I overlook
Evidence set down in the other book.
So they, between the two of them, divide
The single mind where single truths reside.

The Temple of Aphrodite

1

I woke to nobody. Desire. Intent.
And her to follow as embodiment.

2

Twilight. The streets invite me. They run down
Towards the harbour. In the heart of town

Some common land where road and quayside merge.
A kestrel weighs above. On a grass verge

A rabbit, tempted out, soon bobs away.
I drift back to the shopfronts. Now the day

Is switched off, starker lights illumine whores
Who, between open street and shuttered doors,

Poise, whispering incitements. Manliness,
Withdrawn and shy, rises to the caress

Of smooth obscenity, that heady charm,
Which leads me, not to pleasure nor to harm,

But down an inward subway, a deep maze
Of infinitely bifurcating ways.

3

I meet you in a room too dark for shame
And call you Love, who have no other name.

4

Naked, it feels as if some filmy dress
Still clung invisibly to her bare flesh.

It is like language clothed in irony:
Her body – smooth, particular and free –

Is offered in the name of love, might seem
The incarnation of a general dream;

Yet, though I tremble at her skilled caress,
I know I am not the object of address.

5

What you find – making love, with no love meant –
Is contact without cóntent; without contént.

6

An hour before my train. Leaving the car,
I cross the station to a burger bar

That looks out on the street. I sit and read –
Drink tea, drink good strong prose, and do not heed

The garish colours round me or outside
The urgent traffic at its fullest tide.

Combatively my book affirms the good
Of this world's substance – always understood,

First, that the mind which loves the world is more
Than what it loves; and then (in a sense the core

Of such love) that if earthly powers deny
Our love its freedom, we are free to die.

O but it's dark already. Across the way
She stands, under a streetlamp, on display,

A handsome woman, black, in red high heels;
A string vest of the self-same red reveals,

More than it clothes, her breasts' full luxury,
And skin-tight silver ski-pants generously

Outline her other curves, from hip to calf.
I rise, contemplative, then stand and laugh

In the doorway. Words gone, the train can go.
What else in the wide world could move me so?

Amores

I call this latest book Adversity.
Though it is mine, it is obscure to me.
Some passages of love, though, seem more clear
In a dark context, and I gloss them here.

*

It was not quite the last time. Yet, that day,
Orgasm shook my body with a cry
That echoed through me like a long goodbye.
We parted; then you wept, and turned away.

*

We first met maybe seven years ago
But barely more than chatted before this.
Three afternoons of love, and you must go.
I miss you, scarcely knowing whom I miss.

*

Those brieze-block walls: bare in my memory
The room is – basin, bed, one lamp, one chair.
Yet, entering it, I found you also bare,
And lay down in the lap of luxury.

*

Strange that of all things I recall this fact:
Neither the surge of passion nor the act,
But falling asleep like a child no terrors shake,
Who can, because the woman stays awake.

*

Despising though desiring you, I let
Our next date pass, deciding to forget.
I'd known you, say, five hours in fewer days;
Twenty years later, how you touched me stays.

*

I see a broken city in your head
(Beautiful lady) ravaged by cross-fire.
But here, against that backdrop, you are led
By civil urgencies of sweet desire.

*

You speak of hope and liberty, new love.
Why must I speak of loyalty and despair?
Freedom is our two bodies as they move
And hopelessness the passion we must share.

*

I thought myself unscathed, so did not yield,
But ran till, looking back from a safe height,
I saw wrenched bodies on a battlefield
That once had seemed a garden of delight.

*

Dear child, dear lady, bless you where you sleep
Alone, who should be sleeping here with me.
My one desire's that your desire should keep
On beating at the gates of reverie.

Re-reading my Poem 'Saxon Buckle'

My amulet against the shocks of time!
I made it twenty years ago and still
Despair and terror, snared in the taut rhyme,
Are held by that old exercise of skill.

I trawled for meaning in the world out there
From then till now. The changing world's changed me.
And still, through emptiness, my words declare:
'Meaning is ours: in this space you are free.'

Transference

for Graham Davies

A moving tableau, so to speak.
On the same couch, week after week,
Talking of absence, I can see
Its likeness bearing down on me:
The ceiling blankness. But if I
Let my glance fall to where the sky
Through the broad window hangs behind
The web of garden life, I find
Love I'd thought dead diffused among
Bright songbirds; they with inhuman song
And vivid colour, as they feed
At the bird-table, hit my need
For harmony. And then your voice
Behind me, beyond reach of choice,
Speaks out of darkness and dismay.
De profundis, Domine.

The Dream

Under those heads, an argument of coils,
Protean, polymorphous, serpentine.
Hot breath, bared teeth: the questioning is mine,
The questions not. I strike. A neck recoils,

Gives way before my answer. Thus I hack
Into the bloated flesh of it: thus, thus.
Winged helmet, carven shield: the fabulous
Purity, grace and swiftness of attack!

And still the heads. Day breaks. And no respite.
The questions, now I flag, metamorphose,
The asker changes, then the monster goes,

And still the coils are there, a wraith in light.
I rise, I dress for work; blunt sword, cracked shield.
No more than whisper and the worm's revealed.

In the Greenwood

In August 1987, a 27 year-old gun-collector named Michael Ryan shot a young woman dead in Savernake Forest. There was no obvious motive. That same day he killed fifteen other people, including his mother, in the nearby town of Hungerford. He ended by committing suicide.

When Michael Ryan in that forest glade
(Armed and flak-jacketed, his camouflage
Not disentangled quite from leafy shade)
Let out the first spurt of his huge discharge,

He invoked Emptiness: in these dull days
Prince of this land and Regent (for the King
Must brood in exile on our ancient ways
And the green woods of their meandering).

Now, as the echoes die, I hear a man
My countrymen once dreamt of wind his horn –
A note of warning from a vanished wood;

He, gentle yet pugnacious, jovial
And stubbornly enduring, gave up all
His right and fortune to the common good.

1988

The Garden

Efface complexity, forget the bond
Of old affection, trust, ennui...For love,
This room's the world: which all the world beyond,
Although enriched by it, knows nothing of.

Your body is the garden at its heart:
Sweetness and pungency; earth in this place
Is damp, springy with moss, and when I part
The leaves up there, fruit dangles in my face.

Such innocence! But, now you stretch and yawn
And rise, you turn away from me toward
The somewhere-else that is to be endured.
The world is all before us. We shall meet
A messenger with news of our deceit
Where pale flowers shred and tangle on the thorn.

Oasis

The terms of the analogy are strained –
And that is as it should be, for the world
Is nothing but the world and things are called
By names they cannot answer to. Constrained
By what I am to name things, when I see
How beauty proper to a watered place
Extends beyond it to this wilderness
I call this paradise, which it can't be.

And it is paradise I think of too
When your cool body's fluency and grace
Come near, and nearer, in this desert place
As if the Lord were beckoning through you –
   Though God is darkest when his creatures bless
   And paradise is of the wilderness.

The Earth Rising

The men who first set foot on the bleached waste
That is the moon saw rising near in space
A planetary oasis that surpassed
The homesick longings of their voyaging race:

Emerald and ultramarine through a white haze
Like a torn veil – as if no sand or dust
Or stain of spilt blood or invading rust
Corrupted it with reds, browns, yellows, greys.

So visionaries have seen it: to design
Transparent, luminous and, as if new-made,
Cut from surrounding darkness. Praise the Lord,
For *Heaven and earth* (the psalmist sang) *are thine;*
The foundations of the round world thou hast laid,
And all that therein is. And plague and sword.

5
Versions

Caedmon's Hymn

    Now ought we all to sing
    The author of what is –
To hymn his power, invoke his understanding,
    Rehearse his actions, praise him –
        Glorious Father:

    Sing how, as he is God
    Eternal, he became
And is the author of these miracles:
    Who, for the sons of men,
        Made heaven first

    To roof their habitation:
    Whereupon he, the one
Almighty guardian of the tribes of man,
    Made and adorned that too:
        It is the earth.

from Bede's Latin

Canticle of the Sun

O my good Lord, almighty and most high,
Thine are the praise, the honour and the glory
And thereto every blessing.
To thee alone are they due, thee they become,
And worthy is no man to give tongue to thy name.

Praise be to thee, my Lord, with all thou'st made,
And in especial Master Sun, our brother,
Who bringeth day, by whom thou givest light.
Comely he is and bright, of a great shining,
And in thy likeness doth he shape his meaning.

Praise be, my Lord, in Sister Moon and the stars:
In heaven thou mad'st them, costly and bright and fair.

Praise be, my Lord, in Brother Wind and the air
In cloudy and clear sky and in all weathers:
By him thou dost sustain life in thy creatures.

Praise be, my Lord, also in Sister Water,
Who serveth all, lowly and precious and pure.

Praise be, my Lord, also in Brother Fire,
Whereby thou dost illumine the night well,
And he is handsome and jocund, strong and hale.

Praise be, my Lord, in our sister, Mother Earth,
Who nurtureth and governeth us all.
So many kinds of fruit she bringeth forth
With grass and with bright flowers.

Praise be, my Lord, in them who for thy love
Forgive and bear much pain and tribulation.
Blest who bear such in peace, most high,
For by thy hand shall they be crowned in heaven.

Praise be, my Lord, in Sister Death.
None living can escape her.
Woe to all them that die in mortal sin.
Blest whom she findeth in thy holy will –
The second death shall not harm them.

Give thanks to my Lord, bless him, sing his praise,
And serve him humbly all your days.

after St Francis of Assisi

Sestina

I have come now to the long arc of shadow
And the short day, alas, and where the hills
Whiten, the colour gone from the old grass;
Yet my desire is constant in its green,
It has so taken root in the hard stone
That speaks and hears as if it were a woman.

Similarly this miracle of woman
Stays frozen like the deep snow left in shadow:
For she is no more moved than is a stone
By the sweet season – that which warms the hills
Turning the whiteness of them into green
And decking them in wild flowers, herbs and grass.

When her hair is garlanded with woven grass,
She draws the mind away from other women:
She braids the rippling yellow with the green
So beautifully, Love lingers in their shadow –
Love, who confines me here between low hills
More stringently than mortar binding stone.

Her beauty holds more power than precious stones
And nothing remedies – not herb or grass –
The hurt she gives: so over plain and hill
I have fled, my one need to escape that woman,
But from her eyes' clear light have found no shadow
By mountain, wall or leafage dense with green.

There was a time I saw her dressed in green
In such a way she could have made a stone
Feel the great love I bear her very shadow;
I desired her, therefore, in a field of grass –
As much in love as ever any woman
Has been – and ringed about by lofty hills.

But rivers will flow back and climb their hills
Before this wood, which is both damp and green,
Will at my touch catch fire – as fair women
Are known to do; and I would sleep on stone
My whole life long and go feeding on grass
Only to see where her dress casts a shadow.

Whenever the hills cast their blackest shadow,
With lovely green she makes it, this young woman,
Vanish, as stones are hidden in the grass.

after Dante

Dante to Love's Faithful

from the Vita Nuova

To every noble heart these words may move,
Each captive soul that looks into their theme,
I send – to learn how you interpret them –
This greeting in your Lord's name, which is Love.

The stars were shining clear, the starlit hour
Then on the point of passing was the third,
When suddenly Love in his own form appeared;
And to recall that form grips me with horror.

Happy Love seemed: I saw that in one hand
He clutched my heart, while she I love was laid
Across his arms, wrapped in a cloth and sleeping.

Then when he woke her, though she was afraid
He humbly fed the heart to her, which burned:
And as he went away, I saw him weeping.

after Dante

Cavalcanti's Reply

All the nobility men may know on earth,
The joy, the good, it seems to me you saw;
That noble Lord was proving you, whose law
Commands the world of honourable worth.

For where he lives, harsh dreariness must die;
With reason he holds sway in the mind's keep.
No pain he causes when he comes in sleep
Gently to steal our hearts from where we lie.

He stole your heart when she you worship was
Falling – he had perceived it – into death;
And fearing this, he gave it her to eat.

You saw him leave in sorrow then, because
Sweet sleep was on the point of ending with
The imperious advent of its opposite.

after Cavalcanti

Archaic Torso of Apollo

Not to be known, the inconceivable
Head that the eyes ripened in. Yet the torso
Is like a branching gas-lamp, glowing still,
In which his gaze, no more than turned down low,

Burns on, gleams. Else it could not dazzle so,
The curved swell of the chest; nor could there be
In the slight twist of the loins a smile that goes
Toward the fulcrum that was potency.

Else the stone would not stand, disfigured, lopped,
Beneath the shoulders' lucid plunge and rush
And would not glisten like a wild beast's pelt;

And would not from its proper contours thus
Break like a star: for there is nowhere safe
From being seen here. You must change your life.

after Rilke

'Say, poet, what it is you do'

Say, poet, what it is you do. – *I praise.*
How can you look into the monster's gaze
And accept what has death in it? – *I praise.*
But, poet, the anonymous and those
With no name, how do you call on them? – *I praise.*
What right have you though, in each changed disguise,
In each new mask, to trust your truth? – *I praise.*
Both calm and violent things know you for theirs,
Both star and storm: how so? *Because I praise.*

after Rilke

Caedmon of Whitby

A Cantata

The Hymn

Nū scylun hergan   hefanrīcaes Uard,
Metudaes maecti   end his mōdgidanc,
uerc Uuldurfadur,   suē hē uundra gihuaes
ēci Dryctin,   ōr āstelidae.
Hē āērist scōp   aelda barnum
heben til hrofe,   hāleg Scepen.
Thā middungeard   moncynnaes Uard,
ēci Dryctin,   aefter tīadae
firum foldu   Frēa allmectig.

Recitative

There was in the monastery of Whitby a lay brother blessed by God with the gift of song. Indeed, so sweet were his songs that greatly they would inflame the hearts of his hearers, and no other maker could match his cunning. For he learned the art of singing without human instruction, receiving it freely as a gift from God.

Now, although this man dwelt in the monastery many years until he was well-stricken in age, he had at no time learned any songs. And sometimes at table, when the company was set to be merry and had agreed that all should sing, each in his turn, he, when he saw the harp to be coming near him, would rise up before supper was done and go out into the night.

One evening, leaving the feasting-hall in this way, he had gone out to the stable of the beasts, which was to be his care for that whole night. And there, at the fitting hour, he had bestowed his limbs to rest, when suddenly he was aware of one standing before him, who addressed him thus:

Aria

Caedmon, God speed!
Why do you turn aside from your great need?
Why do you stay chaste?
It is not silent plenty but sad waste.
Old man already: when will you begin?
Now, I command you, take up your harp and sing!

Dialogue

Caedmon: I *cannot* sing. Therefore I left the company in the hall – because I do not know how.

Stranger: I tell you you *must* sing to me. Consider no further in your head, but sing as the birds sing.

Caedmon: I have no *matter*. What *words* should I sing, even if there were music in my soul?

Stranger: Sing the beginning of the world: how God made it and the fair creatures that dwell in it.

Aria

What holds me back,
A swimmer,
On the shore?
Would the cold shock
Be more
Than flesh could bear?

Unanswering voice,
Sustainer,
Mighty Lord:
My tuneless speech
Awaits
Your speechless word.

Recitative

So Caedmon began at once to sing, in praise of God, verses which he had never heard before – and sweet was the sound of them. Then his visitor departed from him, and he awoke, and it was day. But sounding yet in his heart was that very song he had sung before in his sleep. And he went at once to beg audience of the Prior, and sang the song to him.

The Hymn

Now should we hail   heaven's guardian,
Praise the Maker,   his might and thought,
The Father of glory,   his work: for he gave
To all wonders   one beginning –
        Everlasting Lord.
First he raised   a roof which is heaven
For the sons of men,   *sanctus artifex*;
And then in time,   everlasting Lord,
Mankind's guardian,   he made earth,
Made and adorned it,   almighty King.

Note

'Caedmon of Whitby' was written as the libretto for John Hopkins's composition *Cantata*, to be broadcast on Radio 3 in 1993. The story comes from the Venerable Bede's *Ecclesiastical History of the English People* and the passages of recitative are loosely based on the sixteenth-century translation of that great book by Thomas Stapleton. The libretto concludes with a version of Caedmon's Hymn, which, dating from the seventh century, is generally regarded as the earliest poem by a known author in any dialect of English. Another version of the same hymn appears on p.69, but this was translated from Bede's Latin prose without reference to the original. 'Invocation' (p.11) also alludes to Caedmon and his hymn.